Grenita Hall's Kitchen:

IT'S SIMPLY DELICIOUS COOKBOOK

Grenita Hall

ISBN: 978-1-955312-72-1

Printed in the United States of America
Story Corner Publishing & Consulting, Inc.
Chesapeake, Virginia
Storycornerpublishing@yahoo.com
www.StoryCornerPublishing.com

Table Of Content

HANDMADE MEAT RECIPES

Maple Beef Sausage

INGREDIENTS

2 Tbs Maple Smoke House Seasoning

2 Tbs Brown Sugar

2 Tbs Dark Brown Sugar

2 Tsp Salt

2 Tsp Dried or Fresh Basil

2 Tsp Cracked Black Pepper

2 Tsp Onion Powder

¼ Tsp Dried Marjoram

½ Tsp Italian Seasoning

1/8 Tsp Crushed Pepper Flakes

3 Lbs Ground Beef

DIRECTIONS

1. Mix all dry seasonings and pepper flakes in a large bowl. Add ground beef to the same bowl and mix well.

2. Cover the bowl and place the meat in the refrigerator for 24 hours. After 24 hours, gather 2 tablespoons of seasoned meat and roll it in a ball. You can smash it into a patty or roll it into a link. It's your choice.

3. In a frying pan add oil and heat on medium heat. Add sausage patties or links and cook for 5-6 minutes on both sides. Remove and allow to cool. Serve and enjoy!

Store excess in the freezer for 2 months in a sealed bag or refrigerator for up to 5 days.

Happy Cooking!

Zesty Turkey Sausage

INGREDIENTS

½ Tsp Italian Seasoning

2 Tbs Sea Salt

2 Tbs Dark Brown Sugar

2 Tsp Dried Sage

2 Tsp Dried Thyme

½ Tsp Dried Marjoram

1 Tsp Ground Black Pepper

1 Tsp Garlic Powder

1 Tsp Onion Powder

1/8 Tsp Ground Clove

1/8 Tsp Nut Meg

1/8 Tsp All Spice

2 Tbs Extra Olive Oil

1/8 Tsp Orange Zest

3 Lbs Ground Turkey

DIRECTIONS

1. Mix all seasonings and orange zest in a large bowl. Add ground turkey to the same bowl and mix well.

2. Cover the bowl and place the meat in the refrigerator for 24 hours. After 24 hours, gather 2 tablespoons of seasoned meat and roll it in a ball. You can smash it into a patty or roll it into a link. It's your choice.

3. In a frying pan add oil and heat on medium heat. Add sausage patties or links and cook for 5-6 minutes on both sides. Remove and allow to cool. Serve and enjoy!

Store excess in the freezer for 2 months in a sealed bag or refrigerator for up to 5 days.

Italian Maple Sage Sausage

INGREDIENTS

2 Tsp Oregano

2 Tsp Basil

½ Tsp Thyme

½ Tsp Rosemary

2 Tbs Minced Garlic

½ Smoked Paprika

½ Tbs Fennel Seeds

1 Tbs Sea Salt

2 Tbs Cracked Black Pepper

½ Teaspoon Cayenne Powder

1 Tbs Dried Parsley

1 Tbs Smoked Maple House Seasoning

1 Tbs Brown Sugar

1/8 Tsp Orange Zest

1/8 Tsp Nut Meg

4Lbs Ground Pork

4 Tbs Olive Oil

DIRECTIONS

1. Mix all seasonings, orange zest, and fennel seeds in a large bowl.

2. Add ground pork in the same bowl and work the seasons into the meat very well.

3. Cover the bowl and place the meat in the refrigerator for 24 hours. After 24 hours, gather 2 tablespoons of seasoned meat and roll it in a ball. You can smash it into a patty or roll it into a link. It's your choice.

4. In a frying pan add oil and heat on medium heat. Add sausage patties or links and cook for 5-6 minutes on both sides. Remove and allow to cool. Serve and enjoy!

Store excess in the freezer for 2 months in a sealed bag or refrigerator for up to 5 days.

Smoked Maple Beef Bacon

INGREDIENTS

4Lbs Beef Belly

½ Cup Curing Salt

3 Tbs Ground Black Pepper

4 Tbs Raw Sugar

½ Tbs Brown Sugar

3 Tbs Pink Himalayan Salt

4 Tbs Pickling Spice

1 Cup Maple Syrup

½ Tsp Thyme

½ Tsp Basil

3 Tbs Olive Oil

Rub:

½ Tsp Granulated Garlic

½ Tsp Crackle Black Pepper

½ Tsp Smoked Maple Mix

DIRECTIONS

1. Add all seasonings and syrup to a large bowl and mix well. Then coat the meat with mixture and place it in a sealed bag. Store it in the refrigerator for five days. After the fifth day, take the meat out of the sealed bag and rinse.

2. In a small bowl add garlic, pepper, and maple mix. Mix well and rub down the meat. Set it aside.

3. Start the smoker and wait until it reaches 150 degrees then add meat. Cook for 3-4 hours. Check the meat every half hour. Remove and allow to cool.

4. Slice meat into thin strips and set aside.

5. In a frying pan add oil and heat on medium heat. Add bacon strips and cook for 3-4 minutes on both sides. Remove and allow to cool. Serve and enjoy!

Store excess in the freezer for 2 months in a sealed bag or refrigerator for up to 5 days.

Maplewood Pork Bacon

INGREDIENTS

1 Skinless Brine Pork Belly

1/3 Cups of Brown Sugar

½ Cup Sea Salt

½ Tsp Ponzu Sauce

¼ Tsp Pink Himalayan Salt

½ Tsp Italian Seasoning

½ Tsp Black Pepper

3 Tbs Avocado Oil

DIRECTIONS

1. Mix seasonings and sauce in a medium bowl, then rub mix all over the meat. Store meat in a sealed bag then sit it in the refrigerator for seven days. After the seventh day take meat out of the sealed bag and rinse.

2. Start the smoker and wait for it to reach (155 F /68 C). Lay pork belly on its side and cook for 3-4 hours. Check the meat every half hour. Remove and allow to cool. Slice meat into thin strips and set aside.

3. In a frying pan add oil and heat on medium heat. Add bacon strips and cook for 3-4 minutes on both sides. Remove and allow to cool. Serve and enjoy!

Store excess in the freezer for 2 months in a sealed bag or refrigerator for up to 5 days.

Plant-Based Vegan Sausage

INGREDIENTS

1Tbs Soy Sauce

¼ Cup Beef Broth

1 Tbs Nutritional Yeast

1 Tbs Vital Wheat Gluten

1 Tbs Oat Flour

½ Tsp Garlic Cloves

½ Tsp Black Pepper

½ Tsp Brown Sugar

½ Tsp Smoked Paprika

½ Tsp Basil

½ Tsp Seasoning Salt

4 Cups Water

3 Tbs Avocado Oil

DIRECTIONS

1. In a medium bowl add all seasonings, soy sauce, wheat, yeast, flour, and beef broth. Mix well with your hands. When the mixture starts to look like thick dough. Roll it into a ball then cut it into four pieces. Then roll each piece into a ball.

2. Separately wrap all four pieces of meat in clear wrap, then a final wrap with aluminum foil. Place all four wrapped pieces into a strainer and cover with a pot lid.

3. In a medium pot add water and bring to a boil. Place the strainer with wrapped meat into the boiling water to steam meat for 10 minutes. Remove the strainer, then place the wrapped meat into the freezer for 3 hours. Remove wrapped meat from the freezer and cut into patties. Set it aside.

4. In a frying pan add oil and heat on medium heat. Add patties and cook For 5-6 minutes on both sides. Remove and allow to cool. Serve & enjoy!

Store excess in the freezer for 2 months in a sealed bag or refrigerator for up to 5 days.

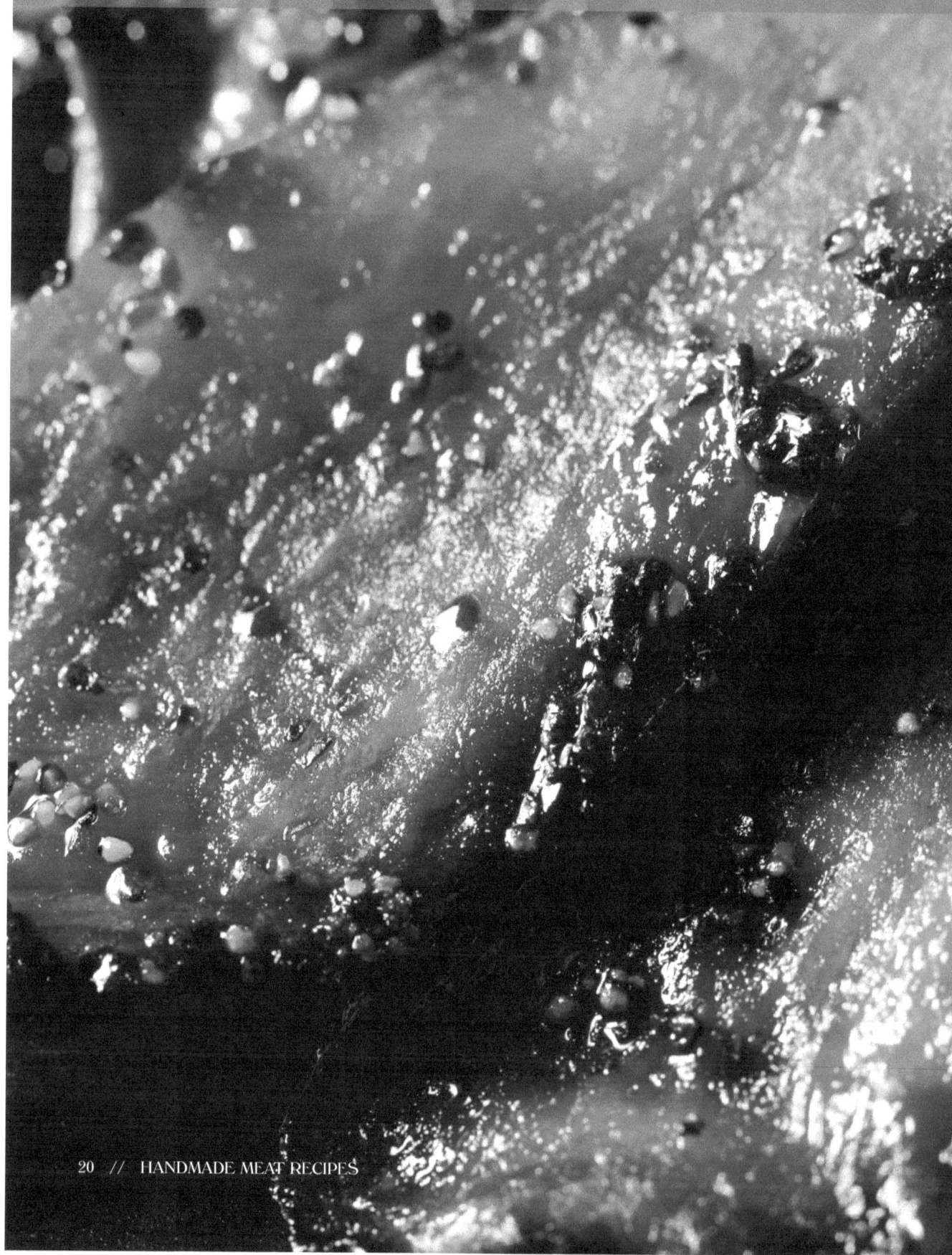

Vegan Maple Bacon

INGREDIENTS

One 9oz package of Tempeh

2 Tbs Soy Sauce

1 Tbs Maple Syrup

2 Tsp Liquid smoke

1 ½ Tsp Maple Blend Syrup

6 Tbs Avocado oil

DIRECTIONS

1. Cut the tempeh into thin slices then place them in a steamer basket over a pot of boiling water. Cover and let steam for 10 minutes. Whisk together soy sauce, liquid smoke, maple syrup, maple blend syrup, and 3 Tbs of avocado oil in a mixing bowl.

2. Add 3 Tbs of avocado oil to a frying pan and heat on medium-high heat. Fry tempeh for 5-6 minutes or until golden brown. Remove and set aside.

3. In the same frying pan add liquid smoke, maple syrup, maple blend syrup, and tempeh. Cook until all the liquid has evaporated from the pan. Move meat back and forward quickly to prevent burning. Remove and place on a paper towel to cool. Serve and enjoy!

Store excess in the freezer for 2 months in a sealed bag or refrigerator for up to 5 days.

Happy Cooking!

SEAFOOD DISHES

Fancy Shrimp & Grits

INGREDIENTS

6 Strips Bacon

3 Cups Chicken Broth

1 Cup Grits

½ Tbs Unsalted Butter

½ Tsp Black Pepper

½ Tsp Sea Salt

1 ½ Cups Mild Cheddar Cheese

½ Lb Large Shrimps

1 Tsp Cajun Seasoning

1 Tsp Old Bay Seasoning

2 Tsp Minced Garlic

½ Tbs Fresh Parsley

½ Chopped Onion

3 Tbs Avocado Oil

DIRECTIONS

1. In a frying pan add avocado oil and heat on medium heat. Add bacon and cook for 5-6 minutes. Remove the bacon and place it on a paper towel to cool. Set bacon grease aside.

2. In a medium pot, add 2 ½ cups of chicken broth and bring to a boil on medium heat. Add grits, black pepper, salt, and unsalted butter to pot and cook for 6-8 minutes. Continually stir grits to prevent lumps and sticking to the bottom of the pot. Once grits are done, add cheese and let simmer for 3 minutes. Then remove from heat and set aside.

3. In a small bowl add shrimp, cajun seasoning, and old bay. Mix well. Heat the same frying pan with the bacon grease and add shrimp. Cook for 6-8 minutes. Remove and set aside on a paper towel to cool.

4. In the same frying pan heat and add garlic and onions to the grease. Cook for 3-4 minutes then add ½ cup of chicken broth to make gravy. Simmer and stir until the mixture is thick enough. Remove and set aside. Serve grits in a bowl and top with shrimp and gravy, then garnish with dried parsley.

Enjoy!

Cajun Fish & Grits

INGREDIENTS

1Lb Catfish Nuggets

1 Cup Louisiana Fish Fry Seasoning

3 Tbs Creole Seasoning

2 Cups Flour

1 Cup Grits

½ Cup Evaporated Milk

2 Tsp Black Pepper

½ Tsp Sea Salt

2 Tbs Unsalted Butter

2 Cups Sharp Cheese

½ Cup Mozzarella Cheese

½ Cup Parmesan Cheese (Grated)

3 ½ Cups Chicken Broth

2 Tbs Avocado Oil

1 Tsp Dried Parsley

DIRECTIONS

1. In a large pot add chicken broth and bring to a boil on medium heat. Add evaporated milk, 1 Tbs black pepper, sea salt, butter, and grits to the same pot and let cook for 20-25 minutes. Then add all the cheeses to the pot and stir to avoid lumping.
Reduce heat and stir until the grits are the desired thickness, then remove from heat and set aside.

2. In a medium bowl add fish, fish fry seasoning, 1 Tbs black pepper, and creole seasoning. Mix well and set aside.

3. In another medium bowl add flour. Dip each piece of fish in flour and cover on both sides. Set aside.

4. In a frying pan add oil and heat on medium heat. Add fish and cook for 3 minutes on both sides. Remove and place on a paper towel to cool. Serve grits in a bowl and place fish on top. Garnish with dried parsley and enjoy.

Cheesy Sausage & Grits

INGREDIENTS

1 Tsp Cajun Seasoning

1 Tsp Island Vibe Seasoning

1 Tsp Old Bay Seasoning

1 Tsp Salt

½ Tbs Grapeseed Oil

½ Tsp Black Pepper

½ Red Bell peppers (Chopped)

½ Orange Bell Pepper (Chopped)

½ Yellow Bell Pepper (Chopped)

1 ½ Onions (Chopped)

2Lbs Baby Shrimps

1 Pack Polish Kielbasa Sausage

1 Cup Chicken Broth

½ Cup Whole Milk

½ Tbs Unsalted Butter

2 Cup Cheddar Cheese

1 Cup Grits

DIRECTIONS

1. In a medium pot add chicken broth and bring to a boil on medium heat. Then add grits, salt, black pepper, milk, and butter. Cook for 10 minutes and stir continually to avoid lumps or sticking to the pot.
Add cheese to grits and allow to simmer for 1-2 minutes. Remove from heat and set aside uncovered to rest.

2. In a frying pan add grapeseed oil and heat on medium heat. Add shrimp, sausage, and the remainder of seasonings to the pan. Cook for 3 minutes on each side. Remove shrimp and sausage from the frying pan and set aside.
Add onions and all bell peppers to the same frying pan, then cook for 2-3 minutes. Remove and set aside.
Serve grits in a bowl with shrimp, sausage, bell peppers, and onions on top, and enjoy!

Grilled Seafood & Grits

INGREDIENTS

1Lbs Salmon

½Lbs Medium Peeled Shrimps

½Lbs Polish Sausage

1 Tsp White Pepper

¼ Tsp Salt

1 Tbs Onion Powder

1 Tbs Garlic Powder

1 Tbs Old Bay

1 Cup Grits

½ Tbs Unsalted Butter

½ Cup Sharp Cheese

2 Cups Chicken Broth

½ Cup Whole Milk

1 Tbs Grapeseed oil

DIRECTIONS

1. In a medium pot add chicken broth and bring to a boil. Add salt, white pepper, milk, butter, and grits. Stir in cheese until it's creamy and smooth. Cook for 10 minutes then remove from heat.

2. Season shrimp and salmon with onion powder, garlic powder, and old bay in a medium bowl.
   In a frying pan add grapeseed oil and heat on medium heat. Add shrimp and cook for 3 minutes on each side. Remove and set aside. In the same frying pan add salmon and cook on each side for 5 minutes. Remove from heat and set aside.

3. Cut sausage into pieces and add to the same frying pan. Cook on each side for 8 minutes. Remove from heat and mix sausage with shrimp and salmon.
   Serve grits in a bowl and add shrimp, sausage, and salmon on top.

Enjoy!

Deep-Fried Stuffed Flounder Crabby Pattie

INGREDIENTS

6 Filets Flounder

1Lb Peeled Medium Shrimp

1 Can Lump Crabmeat

½ Cup Onions

1 Tsp Old Bay Seasoning

1 Tsp Seasoning Salt

1 Tsp Garlic Powder

1 Tsp Italian Seasoning

1 Tsp Dried Parsley

1 Tbs Cream Cheese

1 Tbs Seafood Breadcrumbs

2 Cups Fish Fry Seasoning

2 Cups Avocado Oil

1 Bag of Round Kaiser Rolls

18 Toothpicks

1 Bottle of Russian Dressing

DIRECTIONS

1. In a medium bowl mix together the cream cheese, onions, garlic powder, Italian season, parsley, lump crab meat, and seafood breadcrumbs. Then add the raw shrimp, seasoning salt, and old bay, then mix again and set aside.

2. In a large bowl add fish and fish fry seasoning. Cover fish completely with seasoning.
Lay 3 pieces of fish out on a small baking sheet. Add 3 Tbs of shrimp mixture on top of each piece of fish. Then place another filet on top of the shrimp mixture and hold it together with three toothpicks on each side. Continue this process until all filets are paired together.

3. In a frying pan add avocado oil and heat on medium heat. Add stuffed fish and cook for 3-4 minutes on each side or until golden brown. Remove and allow to cool. Serve and enjoy!

Rich Girl Seafood Sandwich

INGREDIENTS

1Lb Large Peeled Shrimps

½ Stick of Butter

1 Tsp Seasoning Salt

½ Tbs Flour

½ Tbs Cornmeal

½ Tbs Black Pepper

1 Tsp Garlic Powder

1 Tsp Dried Parsley

1 Egg

½ Cup Buttermilk

1 Tsp Hot Sauce

1 Tbs Old Bay

3 Cups Avocado Oil

1 Bag Amoroso's Club Rolls

1 Romaine Lettuce (Chopped)

1 Sliced Tomato

1 Bottle of Russian Dressing

DIRECTIONS

1. In a small bowl add butter milk, egg, and hot sauce then mix well and set aside.
   Add flour, cornmeal, garlic powder, seasoning salt, and parsley in a medium bowl then mix and set aside.
   In another medium bowl add shrimp, black pepper, and old bay then mix.

2. Add shrimps one by one to the butter milk mixture then add shrimps to the flour mixture and lay each on a cookie sheet.
   Place the cookie sheet in the refrigerator for 10 minutes.

3. In a frying pan add oil and heat on medium heat. Add shrimp and cook on both sides for 3 minutes. Remove and place on a paper towel to cool.

4. Add butter to the frying pan and toast the rolls. Remove the rolls then add Russian dressing, lettuce, tomatoes, and shrimp to the rolls. Serve and enjoy.

Ramen Seafood Boil

INGREDIENTS

1Lb Peeled Shrimps
1Lb Green Shell Mussels
1Lb Snow Crabs
1 Pack Wagyu Beef Sausage
2 Packs of Ramen Noodles
1 ½ Stick Unsalted Butter
½ Green Bell Pepper (Diced)
½ Red Bell Pepper (Diced)
½ Orange Bell Pepper (Diced)
½ Cup Onions (Diced)
½ Tbs Minced Garlic
1 Boiled Egg
½ Tsp Garlic Powder
½ Tsp Lemon Pepper
½ Tbs Onion Powder
½ Tsp Paprika
1 Tbs Old Bay
1 Tbs Brown Sugar
1 Tbs Zatarain's Crab Boil Seasoning
1 Tsp Hot Sauce
1 Lemon (Squeezed)
2 ½ Cups Seafood Stock
1 Tsp White Vinegar
1 Tbs Avocado Oil
1 Can Sweet Corn
3 Cup Water

DIRECTIONS

1. Add all diced vegetables to a medium bowl and set aside. Slice sausage into chunks and set aside in another medium bowl.
Add all seasonings and shrimp to the same bowl with sausage. Mix well and set aside.

2. In a medium pot add seafood stock, hot sauce, lemon juice, vinegar, and snow crabs. Cook for 5 minutes and let simmer for 5-10 minutes. Then remove snow crabs from the pot and set aside.
In the same pot, add ½ stick of butter to the stock mixture and bring to a boil. Add mussels and cook for 10 minutes, then remove from pot and set aside. Save the stock mixture!

3. In a frying pan add ½ stick of butter and heat on medium heat. Add sausages and cook for 5-7 minutes or until cooked all the way through. Remove from pan and set aside.
Add shrimp and avocado oil to the same frying pan and cook for 4-5 minutes. Remove from pan and set aside.

4. In a medium pot add ½ stick of butter, 1 cup of water, bell peppers, onions, minced garlic, and sweet corn. Cook for 3-5 minutes then remove and set aside.

5. In the same pot as the stock mixture, add 2 cups of water and bring to a boil. Add 2 packs of ramen noodles and cook for 2-4 minutes. Then remove the pot from the heat.
Serve noodles, vegetables, shrimp, sausage, mussels, boiled egg, and 1-2 cups of stock in a bowl with snow crabs on the side.

Enjoy!

Bang Bang Shrimp & Rice

INGREDIENTS

1Lb Large Peeled Shrimps

1 Tsp Seasoning Salt

1 Tsp Fish Seasoning

1 Tsp Black Pepper

1 Tsp Garlic Powder

2 Egg Yolks

1 Tsp Old Bay Seasoning

1 Cup Flour

½ Tsp Cornstarch

½ Tbs All Purpose Seasoning

1 Tsp Paprika

2 Tbs Avocado Oil

2 Cups Jasmine Rice

4 Cups Water

Sauce:

4 Tbs Mayo

½ Cup Chili Sauce

1 Tsp Soy Sauce

1 Tsp Paprika

1 Tbs Honey

DIRECTIONS

1. Mix all sauce ingredients in a small bowl and set aside in the refrigerator for 15 minutes.

2. In a medium bowl mix the flour, cornstarch, black pepper, all-purpose seasoning, garlic powder, and paprika, then set aside.
In a small bowl beat egg yolks and set aside.

3. In a frying pan add avocado oil and set on medium heat.
Season shrimp with old bay, fish seasoning, and seasoning salt. Then dip shrimp in egg yolk and quickly cover both sides in flour mixture.
Cook shrimp for 3 minutes on each side and remove from pan.

4. Add water to a medium pot and bring to a boil. Add rice and boil for about 5 minutes. Serve rice in a bowl with shrimp and sauce on top.

Happy Cooking!

Seafood Feast Spaghetti

INGREDIENTS

1Lb Ground Beef
1Lb Peeled Shrimps
3 Cups Lump Crabmeat
1 Box Spaghetti
1 Red Onion (Diced)
½ Red Bell Pepper (Diced)
½ Green Bell Pepper (Diced)
2 Tbs Garlic Powder (Diced)
1 Tbs Onion Powder
1 Tsp Crushed Red Pepper Flacks
2 Tbs Worcestershire Sauce
2 Tbs Granulated Sugar
1 Tbs Dried Parsley
1 Tbs Italian Seasoning
1 Tsp Salt
1 Tsp Black Pepper
1 Tbs Old Bay Seasoning
3 Cup Water
½ Cup Dried Basil
2 Tbs Grapeseed Oil
1 Tbs Old Bay Seasoning
15oz Tomato Sauce
6oz Tomato Paste
1 Can Diced Tomatoes

DIRECTIONS

1. In a medium bowl add ground beef, onions, bell peppers, onion powder, and Italian seasoning. Mix well and set aside.
In a frying pan add 1 Tbs oil and heat on medium heat. Add ground beef mixture and cook for 5-7 minutes, then drain excess oil and set aside.

2. In a medium pot on low heat, add ground beef mixture, all tomato sauces, pepper flacks, parsley, black pepper, basil, worcestershire, and sugar, then stir well. Allow to simmer for 3-4 minutes, then remove from heat and set aside.

3. In another medium pot add water and bring to a boil. Add spaghetti and salt. Boil for 4-5 minutes then remove from water and rinse with cool water.

4. In a frying pan add 1 Tbs oil and heat on medium heat. Add shrimp, crabmeat, and old bay seasoning. Cook for 3-4 minutes on both sides then remove and add shrimp to pot with ground beef mixture. Mix well.
Serve spaghetti in a bowl and add sauce mixture on top.

Happy Cooking!

Shrimpy Shrimp Burgers

INGREDIENTS

5 Tbs Butter
1Lb Peeled Medium Shrimp (Cut in half)
1 Egg
¼ Cup Panko Breadcrumbs
1 ½ Tsp Salt
2 Tbs Old Bay Seasoning
1 Tsp Lemon Zest
½ Cup Mayo
1 Tsp Hot Sauce
1 Tbs Lemon Juice
1 ½ Tbs Old Bay
3 Hamburger Rolls
1 Tbs Mustard
1 Cup Shredded Lettuce
6 Slices of Tomatoes

DIRECTIONS

1. Place 3 Tbs butter in a large microwavable bowl and melt in the microwave for about 25 seconds. Add egg and beat until mixed well then add shrimp to mixture. Mix in shrimp well and set aside.

2. In a medium bowl add shrimp mix, panko breadcrumbs, 1 Tsp salt, 1 Tbs old bay, lemon zest, and ½ Tbs lemon juice. Mix well and set aside.

3. Place parchment paper on a cookie sheet and set aside.
   Shape shrimp mix into patties (3 ½ -inch) and place on cookie sheet. Cover patties and place in refrigerator for 15 minutes.

4. In a separate bowl, mix mayo, mustard, hot sauce, ½ Tbs of lemon juice, ½ Tsp salt, and ½ Tbs old bay seasoning. Set it aside.

5. In a frying pan add 2 Tbs butter and place over medium heat.
   Add shrimp patties and cook on each side for 5-6 minutes.
   Remove patties from pan and place on hamburger rolls. Add mayo mix, lettuce, and tomatoes, and enjoy!

Sizzling Lobster Cheeseburger

INGREDIENTS

4 Lobster Tails

1 Tbs Old Bay Seasoning

2 Tbs Black Pepper

1 Tbs Garlic Powder

1 Tbs Season Salt

1 Tbs Salt

2 Egg whites

1 Cup Saltine Crackers

1 Cup Breadcrumbs

1Lb Ground Steak

½ Cup Flour

4 Tbs Olive Oil

1 Tbs Butter

1 Cup Mozzarella Cheese

½ Tsp Dried Parsley

1 Bottle of Russian dressing
or KRAFT tartar sauce

3 Hawaiian Burger Rolls

1 Cup Shredded Lettuce

1 Sliced Tomato

DIRECTIONS

1. Split lobster tails in half.
   Wash them, pat dry, and season them with seasoning salt, 1 Tbs black pepper, old bay seasoning, and garlic powder.

2. In a medium bowl, beat egg whites well and set aside.
   Add flour to another medium bowl, then set aside.

3. Add crackers and breadcrumbs into a blender and mix until crushed fine.
   Pour into a third medium bowl and set aside.

4. Add ground steak, salt, and 1 Tbs black pepper into a medium bowl. Mix well.
   Shape the steak mixture into patties and set aside.

5. Heat a skillet pan and add 2 Tbs olive oil.
   Dip lobster tails one at a time in flour, then egg white mix, then cracker mix, and into the skillet to cook for 4-5 minutes.
   Remove lobster tails from the skillet and set aside.

6. In another skillet add 2 Tbs oil and heat on medium heat. Add steak burgers and cook for 5-6 minutes.
   Remove from skillet and place on a paper towel.

7. Toast rolls then add butter, lettuce, tomatoes, cheese, lobster tail, and dressing.

Enjoy!

Grenita's Catfish Sandwich

INGREDIENTS

4 Filet Catfish
2 Cups Fish Fry Batter
2 Eggs
1 Tsp Seasoning Salt
1 Tsp Black Pepper
1 Tsp Paprika
1 Tsp Garlic Powder
1 Tsp Onion Powder
1 Tsp Italian Seasoning
3 Tbs Avocado Oil
1 Tbs Butter
3 Long Bread Rolls
1 Cup Sliced Red Onions
1 Sliced Tomato
1 Cup Shredded Lettuce
1 Cup Sliced Pickles
1 Bottle of Russian dressing

DIRECTIONS

1. In a medium bowl add seasoning salt, black pepper, paprika, garlic powder, and Italian seasoning.
   Add fish fry batter to another medium bowl. In a third medium bowl add eggs and lightly beat.

2. Add oil to a skillet and heat.
   Dip each piece of fish into the bowl with the seasoning, then the egg mix, and lastly into the fish fry batter.

3. Once each piece of fish is dipped, place it in the skillet and cook for 5 minutes on each side.

4. Remove from skillet and place on a paper towel to cool.
   Then add onions to skillet and sauté for 1-2 minutes.

5. In another skillet add butter and toast rolls for 3-4 seconds.
   Place fish, lettuce, tomatoes, onions, and dressing or tartar sauce on rolls.

Serve and enjoy!

CHICKEN DISHES

Baked Barbecue Chicken

INGREDIENTS

1Lb Chicken Thighs

1 Bottle of Barbecue Sauce

1 ½ Cup Olive Oil

½ Tbs Season Salt

½ Tbs Garlic Powder

½ Tbs Onion Powder

½ Tbs Paprika

½ Tbs Parsley

½ Tsp Basil

DIRECTIONS

1. Preheat oven to 365 degrees and line a large baking pan with foil.

2. Season chicken with all seasonings from the ingredient list.

3. Oil the baking pan and lay the chicken on the pan. Place pan in oven and bake for 30-45 minutes.
   Remove and cover chicken in barbecue sauce. Then allow it to sit for 10 minutes.

Enjoy!

Lemon Pepper Chicken Over Brown Rice

INGREDIENTS

½ Lb Chicken Wing

1 Tbs Lemon Pepper Seasoning

1 Tbs Black Pepper

1 Tbs Onion Powder

1 Tbs Garlic Powder

1 Tbs Paprika

½ Cup Olive Oil

1 Tbs Parsley

1 Tbs Basil

1 Cup Brown Rice

½ Stick Butter

1 ½ Cups Water

DIRECTIONS

1. Preheat the oven to 365 degrees.

2. Mix all seasonings and oil in a medium bowl. Add chicken and coat well. Place chicken in an aluminum pan and cover with foil.

3. Allow chicken to bake for a half hour covered and one hour uncovered. Then remove from oven.

4. In a medium pot add 1½ cups of water, 1 teaspoon of salt, and butter. Bring to a boil then add rice. Cover, but leave the lid open just a little. Cook for 25-30 minutes then set aside.

5. Serve chicken and rice together and enjoy!

Lemon Pepper Barbecue Chicken

INGREDIENTS

1Lb Chicken Wings

1 Bottle BBQ Sauce

1 Tbs Seasoning Salt

1 Tbs Garlic Powder

1 Tbs Black Pepper

1 Tbs Lemon Pepper Seasoning

1 Tbs Parsley

1 Tbs Italian Seasoning

½ Cup Olive Oil

Non-Stick Cooking Spray

DIRECTIONS

1. Preheat the oven to 365 degrees. Then line a large baking pan with foil and set it aside.

2. Mix all seasonings and oil in a medium bowl. Add chicken and coat well. Coat the bottom of the foiled pan with non-stick cooking spray and place chicken in it. Cover the top of the pan with foil and place in the oven.

3. Allow chicken to bake for a half hour covered and one hour uncovered. Then remove from oven.

4. Coat chicken with barbecue sauce and allow it to sit for about 10 minutes. Then serve with your favorite side dish.

Enjoy!

Baked Jerk Chicken

INGREDIENTS

1Lb Chicken Wings

1 Bottle of Mild Jerk Marinade

½ Cup Browning Sauce

½ Tbs Garlic Powder

½ Tbs Onion Powder

½ Tbs Paprika

½ Tbs Brown Sugar

½ Tbs Black Pepper

½ Cup Mild Jerk Seasoning

1 Tsp White Vinegar

½ Tbs Parsley

½ Tbs Basil

½ Cup Ketchup

1 Tsp Seeded Peppers

½ Cup Olive Oil

DIRECTIONS

1. Place all seasonings and oil in a large bowl. Add chicken and coat well.

2. In another bowl, add the browning sauce, mild jerk marinade sauce, vinegar, and brown sugar then mix well. Place seasoned chicken in the mixture one at a time and rub the mixture into each piece. Leave the chicken in the bowl and cover. Place the bowl in the refrigerator for 20-30 minutes.

3. Preheat oven to 365 degrees and place chicken on a baking pan. Do not add water, or oil, or cover the baking pan. Bake for 30 minutes on each side. Remove from oven and coat chicken with ketchup and juice from the bottom of the pan.
Place back in the oven for 10 minutes. Remove and let cool.
Serve and enjoy with your favorite sides!

Baked Curry Chicken

INGREDIENTS

1Lb Chicken Thighs

½ Cup Curry Powder Seasoning

½ Tbs Black Pepper

½ Tbs Garlic Powder

½ Tbs Onion Powder

½ Tsp Cumin Seasoning

½ Tsp Seasoning Salt

½ Cup Olive Oil

1 Tbs Basil

½ Cup Chicken Broth

DIRECTIONS

1. Preheat the oven to 365 degrees and add chicken broth to a large baking pan, then set aside.

2. Mix all seasonings and oil in a medium bowl. Add chicken and coat well.

3. Place chicken in the baking pan and allow the chicken to bake for a half hour covered and one hour uncovered. Then remove from oven and let cool.

Serve and enjoy!

Smoked Rotisserie Chicken

INGREDIENTS

1Lb Whole Chicken

½ Tbs Brown Sugar

½ Tbs Black Pepper

½ Tbs Garlic Powder

½ Tbs Onion Powder

½ Tbs Paprika

½ Tbs Basil

½ Tbs Parsley

½ Tbs Seasoning Salt

1 Tsp Chicken seasoning

2 Tbs Avocado Oil

DIRECTIONS

1. Preheat the oven to 365 degrees.

2. Mix all seasonings and oil in a medium bowl. Then coat the chicken well with the mixture.

3. Tie chicken legs together with the cooking string. Cover a large roasting pan with foil and place chicken into the pan. Bake for 30-45 minutes or until chicken is done. Remove from oven and let cool.

Happy Cooking!

Simply Delicious Orange Tangy Chicken

INGREDIENTS

1Lb Party Wings

1 Cup Orange Juice (Fresh Squeeze)

½ Tbs Fresh Ginger

2 Grated Garlic Glove

1 Tsp Salt

1 Tsp Black Pepper

4 Tbs All-Purpose Flour

1 Tbs Cornstarch

1 Cup Water

1 Tbs Paprika

½ Cup Brown Sugar

1 Tbs Honey

2 Tbs Soy Sauce

2 Tbs White Vinegar

½ Cup Avocado Oil

DIRECTIONS

1. Mix salt, black pepper, ginger, garlic, and ½ cup orange juice in a medium bowl. Add chicken and coat well with the seasonings. Leave the seasoned chicken in the bowl and cover. Place in the refrigerator for 25 minutes.

2. Preheat the skillet on low heat and add oil. Mix water, flour, and cornstarch in a medium bowl. Remove chicken from the refrigerator then add flour mixture to the same bowl. Mix well and set aside.

3. In a small bowl, create sauce by adding paprika, brown sugar, honey, soy sauce, vinegar, and ½ cup orange juice. Mix well and set aside.

4. Turn skillet heat up to medium heat and add chicken. Do not overcrowd the pan. Cook for 20-30 minutes.

5. In another pan add sauce mix and bring to a boil. When the sauce starts to thicken, add chicken and cook for 3-5 minutes. Then remove from pan and let cool.

Serve and enjoy!

Hickory Baked Smoked Chicken

INGREDIENTS

1Lb Chicken Wings

1 Tbs Seasoning Salt

1 Tbs Garlic Powder

1 Tbs Crushed Fresh Garlic

3 Tbs Brown Sugar

1 Tsp Cinnamon

1 Tsp Parsley

1 Tsp Basil

1 Bottle of BBQ Sauce

1 Tsp Worcestershire Sauce

2 Pinches Cayenne Pepper

1 Tbs Barbecue Rum

DIRECTIONS

1. Preheat oven to 375 degrees, grease the baking pan, and set aside.

2. In a small bowl mix all dry ingredients and worcestershire sauce together well. Coat chicken in mixture and place in baking pan for 40 minutes.

3. Brush barbecue sauce onto the chicken, turn the heat down to 165 degrees and bake for another 10 minutes. Remove, let cool, and enjoy!

Old Bay Honey Chicken

INGREDIENTS

4 Boneless Chicken Breast

½ Tbs Old Bay Seasoning

1 Tsp Baking Powder

1 Tbs Seasoning Salt

1 Tbs Black Pepper

1 Tbs Garlic Powder

DIRECTIONS

1. Preheat oven to 400 degrees and line a baking sheet with foil.

2. Mix dry seasonings and baking powder well. Rub mixture onto chicken breast one at a time and lay on the baking sheet. Bake for 30 minutes then turn the chicken over and bake at 420 degrees for another 30 minutes. Allow to cool and enjoy.

General Tso's Chicken

INGREDIENTS

2 Boneless Skinless Chicken Breast

½ Cup Cornstarch

2 Tbs Cornstarch

2 Tbs Rice Vinegar

2 Tbs Soy Sauce

2 Tbs Hoisin Sauce

1 Tbs Brown Sugar

1 Tbs Seasoning Salt

1 Tbs Black Pepper

½ Cup Olive Oil

1 Tbs Fresh Garlic

1 Seeded Pepper

1 Tsp Ginger

½ Cup Water

DIRECTIONS

1. In a medium bowl add seasoning salt, black pepper, and 2 Tbs cornstarch. Mix well. Add chicken to the bowl and coat well.

2. Heat a frying pan and add olive oil. Add chicken and fry until golden brown, then remove.

3. In a medium pot add garlic, seeded pepper, ginger, soy sauce, hoisin sauce, and rice vinegar. Bring to boil on medium heat then add ½ cup cornstarch and water.

4. Stir until it begins to thicken then add chicken. Cook on medium heat for another 15 minutes then let cool and serve.

Soul Fried Chicken

INGREDIENTS

1Lb Chicken Quarter Leg

2 Tbs Seasoning Salt

2 Tbs Black Pepper

2 Tbs Garlic Powder

2 Tbs Onion Powder

2 Tbs Paprika

2 Tbs Hot Sauce

2 Tbs Parsley

2 Cups Olive Oil

2 Cups All-Purpose flour

DIRECTIONS

1. Mix all seasonings in a medium bowl. Add chicken and coat well.

2. Heat frying pan on medium heat and add olive oil.

3. In another medium bowl add flour and place seasoned chicken into flour. Shake off excess flour and place chicken in a frying pan one at a time.

4. Fry chicken on each side for 5-10 minutes or when golden brown. Allow to cool and enjoy.

Tasty Fried Korean Chicken

INGREDIENTS

3 Chicken Breast (Cut into cubes)

1 Cup Cornstarch

¼ Cup Flour

½ Tbs Black Pepper

½ Tbs Salt

1 Tbs Seasoning Salt

2 Eggs

1 Cup Avocado Oil

Sauce:

¼ Cup Ketchup

4 Tbs Chili Sauce

¼ Cup Honey

3 Tbs Brown Sugar

½ Cup Soya Sauce

½ Cup Water

2 Minced Garlic Cloves

1 Tsp Red Pepper Flakes

1 Tbs Cornstarch

2 Tsp Sesame Oil

DIRECTIONS

1. In a medium bowl add sauce ingredients and mix well. Set it aside.

2. In another medium bowl add flour, cornstarch, seasoning salt, salt, and black pepper.
   In a third medium bowl add eggs and beat well.

3. Heat a frying pan on medium heat and add avocado oil.

4. Place chicken in the egg wash bowl a little at a time and coat well, then remove and add the chicken to the flour mix bowl. Repeat the process until all chicken has been added to the egg wash and flour mixture.

5. Add battered chicken to the frying pan and cook on both sides for 5-10 minutes. Remove from heat and set aside.

6. In a medium pan add the sauce ingredients and bring to a boil for 1 minute. Add chicken to sauce and stir until all chicken is coated well. Let cool and serve.

GOURMET SALAD RECIPES

Fried Flounder Salad

INGREDIENTS

1Lb Flounder

1 Cucumber

½Lb Cherry Tomatoes

1 Red Onion

1 Bag Romaine Lettuce

4 Tbs Olive Oil

1 Tbs Seasoning Salt

1 Tbs Garlic Powder

1 Pack Fish Fry Mix

Salad Dressing of Choice

DIRECTIONS

1. Heat frying on medium heat and add olive oil.

2. In a medium bowl add seasoning salt, garlic powder, fish fry mix, and fish. Coat fish well.

3. Add fish to frying pan and cook for 8 minutes on both sides. Remove from heat and place fish on a paper towel or cooling rack.

4. Cut up all the vegetables and mix in a large bowl. Add fried flounder on top of salad and salad dressing of choice.

Enjoy!

Grilled Salmon Salad

INGREDIENTS

2Lb Salmon

½Lb Cherry Tomatoes

1 Cucumber

1 Boiled Egg

1 Bag of Roman Lettuce

1 Green Bell Pepper

1 Red Bell Pepper

1 Orange Bell Pepper

1 Can Black Beans

1 Can Sweet Corn

½ Stick Butter

½ Tsp Garlic Powder

1 Tsp Seasoning Salt

1 Tsp Onion Powder

2 Tbs Olive Oil

Salad Dressing of Choice

DIRECTIONS

1. Heat frying on medium heat and add olive oil.

2. In a medium bowl add seasoning salt, garlic powder, and fish. Coat fish well.

3. Add fish to frying pan and cook for 4-5 minutes on both sides. Remove from heat and place fish on cooling rack.

4. Cut up all the vegetables and mix in a large bowl. Then set aside.

5. In a small pot add black beans, sweet corn, butter, and onion powder. Cook for 3-5 minutes and remove from heat and drain.

6. Add beans, corn, boiled egg, salmon, and salad dressing of your choice to the salad.

Enjoy!

Salmon & Shrimp Salad

INGREDIENTS

½Lb Medium Shelled Shrimps

1Lb Salmon

1 Cucumber

1 Boiled Egg

1 Red Bell Pepper

1 Orange Bell Pepper

1 Red Onion

1 Bag of Roman Lettuce

½ Tsp Seasoning Salt

½ Tsp Garlic Powder

2 Tbs Olive Oil

Salad Dressing of Choice

DIRECTIONS

1. Heat frying on medium heat and add olive oil.

2. In a medium bowl add seasoning salt, garlic powder, shrimp, and fish. Coat fish and shrimp well.

3. Add fish to frying pan and cook for 4-5 minutes on both sides. Remove from heat and place fish on cooling rack. Add shrimp to frying pan and cook for 2-3 minutes. Remove from heat and place on cooling rack.

4. Cut up all the vegetables and mix in a large bowl. Add salmon, shrimp, boiled egg, and salad dressing of choice.

Happy Cooking!

Grilled Teriyaki Salmon & Shrimp Salad

INGREDIENTS

1Lb Salmon

½Lb Large Shelled Shrimps

1 Boiled Egg

1 Cucumber

1 Bag of Roman Lettuce

1 Red Onion

½Lb Red Cherry Tomatoes

1 Green Bell Pepper

2 Tbs Olive Oil

1 Tsp Garlic Powder

1 Tsp Seasoning Salt

4 Tbs Teriyaki Sauce

Salad Dressing of Choice

DIRECTIONS

1. Heat frying on medium heat and add olive oil.

2. In a medium bowl add seasoning salt, garlic powder, shrimp, and fish. Coat fish and shrimp well.

3. Add fish and 2 Tbs of teriyaki sauce to the frying pan and cook for 4-5 minutes on both sides. Remove from heat and place fish on cooling rack. Add shrimp and 2 Tbs of teriyaki sauce to the frying pan and cook for 2-3 minutes. Remove from heat and place on cooling rack.

4. Cut up all the vegetables and mix in a large bowl. Add salmon, shrimp, boiled egg, and salad dressing of choice.

Enjoy!

Teriyaki Salmon Salad

INGREDIENTS

1Lb Salmon

1 Cucumber

1 Boiled Egg

1 Red Onion

½Lb Cherry Tomatoes

1 Sweet Yellow Pepper

1 Bag Lettuce

1 Tbs Seasoning Salt

1 Tbs Garlic Powder

2 Tbs Olive Oil

3 Tbs Teriyaki Sauce

Salad Dressing of Choice

DIRECTIONS

1. Heat frying on medium heat and add olive oil.

2. In a medium bowl add seasoning salt, garlic powder, and fish. Coat fish well.

3. Add fish and teriyaki sauce to the frying pan and cook for 4-5 minutes on both sides. Remove from heat and place fish on cooling rack.

4. Cut up all the vegetables and mix in a large bowl. Add salmon, boiled egg, and salad dressing of choice.

Happy Cooking!

Teriyaki Flounder Salad

INGREDIENTS

1Lb Flounder

1 Cucumber

½Lb Cherry Tomatoes

1 Bag Romaine Lettuce

1 Red Onion

1 Red Bell Pepper

1 Orange Bell Pepper

4 Tbs Olive Oil

1 Tbs Seasoning Salt

1 Tbs Garlic Powder

½ Salt

1 Can Sweet Corn

½ Stick Butter

1 Tbs Black Pepper

1 Bag Fish Fry Seasoning

3 Tbs Teriyaki Sauce

Salad Dressing of Choice

DIRECTIONS

1. Heat frying on medium heat and add olive oil.

2. In a medium bowl add seasoning salt, garlic powder, black pepper, fish fry seasoning, and fish. Coat fish well.

3. Add fish and teriyaki sauce to the frying pan and cook for 8 minutes on both sides. Remove from heat and place fish on cooling rack.

4. Add corn, salt, and butter to a small pot. Cook for 2-3 minutes and remove from heat and drain.

5. Cut up all the vegetables and mix in a large bowl. Add flounder, corn, and salad dressing of choice.

Enjoy!

Fried Honey Buffalo Chicken Salad

INGREDIENTS

3 Chicken Breast

1 Bag Romaine Lettuce

½Lb Cherry Tomatoes

2 Tbs Honey

½ Cup All-Purpose Flour

1 Tbs Seasoning Salt

1 Tbs Black Pepper

2 Tbs Garlic Powder

½ Cup Grapeseed Oil

1 Cucumber

1 Boiled Egg

4 Tbs Hot Sauce

½ Stick Butter

Salad Dressing of Choice

DIRECTIONS

1. Heat frying on medium heat and add grapeseed oil.

2. In a medium bowl add seasoning salt, black pepper, 1 Tbs garlic powder, flour, and chicken. Coat chicken well.

3. Add chicken to the frying pan and cook for 6-8 minutes on both sides. Remove from heat and place chicken on cooling rack.

4. In a small pot add butter, hot sauce, honey, and 1 Tbs garlic powder. Simmer for 1-2 minutes and add cooked chicken to the sauce. Simmer for another 1-2 minutes then remove.

5. Cut up all the vegetables and mix in a large bowl. Add chicken, boiled egg, and salad dressing of choice.

Enjoy!

Zesty Tuna Salad

INGREDIENTS

1 Bag Romaine Lettuce

1 Cucumber

½Lb Cherry Tomatoes

1 Boiled Egg (Diced)

2 Cans of Tuna Fish

2 Tbs Sweet Relish

½ Yellow Onion

½ Tsp Dijon Mustard

2 Tbs Mayonnaise

1 Cup Celery (Diced)

1 Tbs Salt

1 Tbs Pepper

1 Tsp Sugar

Salad Dressing of Choice

DIRECTIONS

1. In a medium bowl add tuna, salt, black pepper, sugar, relish, mustard, egg, celery, onion, and mayonnaise. Mix well.

2. Cut up all the vegetables and mix in a large bowl. Add tuna mix and salad dressing of choice.

Enjoy!

Macaroni Chicken Salad

INGREDIENTS

1 Box Macaroni

3 Chicken Breast

½ Red Onion (Diced)

½ Green Bell Pepper (Diced)

3 Tbs Relish

1 Boiled Egg

4 Tbs Mayonnaise

½ Tbs Dijon Mustard

½ Tsp Celery Seeds

1 Tsp Seasoning Salt

2 Tsp Black Pepper

1 Tsp Sugar

½ Tsp Paprika

2 Tsp Salt

2 ½ Cups Water

½ Cup Olive Oil

DIRECTIONS

1. In a medium pot add water and 1 Tsp salt, then bring to a boil. Add macaroni and cook for 7-8 minutes. Remove from heat and strain under cold water. Then set aside.

2. In a medium bowl add chicken, ½ Tsp seasoning salt, 1 Tsp black pepper, and paprika. Mix well.

3. In a frying pan heat on low heat and add olive oil. Add chicken to frying pan and cook for 5-8 minutes on each side then remove and place chicken on a plate covered with a paper towel. Allow to cool then dice chicken.

4. In a medium bowl add diced egg, pepper, onion, and chicken. Then add macaroni, mustard, mayonnaise, celery seeds, sugar, relish, 1 Tsp salt, 1 Tsp black pepper, and ½ Tsp seasoning salt. Mix well and enjoy.

Garden Chicken Salad

INGREDIENTS

3 Skinless Chicken Breast

1 Bag Romaine Lettuce

½Lb Cherry Tomatoes

1 Cucumber

½ Red Onion

½ Red Bell Peppers

½ Orange Bell Peppers

1 Can Black Beans

1 Tbs Seasoning Salt

1 Tbs Black Pepper

1 Tbs Garlic Powder

1 Tbs Onion Powder

1 Boiled Egg

½ Stick Butter

½ Cup Grapeseed Oil

Salad Dressing of Choice

DIRECTIONS

1. In a medium bowl add chicken and seasonings. Mix well.

2. In a frying pan heat on low heat and add oil. Add chicken to frying pan and cook for 5-8 minutes on each side then remove and place chicken on a plate covered with a paper towel. Allow to cool then cut chicken strips.

3. In a small pot add butter and beans. Cook for 2-4 minutes, then remove and drain.

4. In a medium bowl add vegetables, diced egg, beans, chicken, and salad dressing of your choice. Mix well and enjoy!

Sweet & Tangy Pasta Salad

INGREDIENTS

1 Box of Macaroni

½ Green Bell Peppers

½ Red Bell Peppers

½ Orange Bell Peppers

½Lb Tomatoes

1 Cucumber

½ Red Onion

1 Tbs Sugar

½ Tsp Seasoning Salt

½ Tsp Black Pepper

½ Tsp Celery Seeds

1 Pinch of Cayenne Pepper

1 Tbs Salt

½ Stick Butter

1 Can Black Beans

1 Can Sweet Corn

½ Cup Zesty Italian Dressing

½ Tsp Ranch Dressing

DIRECTIONS

1. In a medium pot add water and salt, then bring to a boil. Add macaroni and cook for 7-8 minutes. Remove from heat and strain under cold water. Then set aside.

2. In a small pot add beans, corn, butter, celery seeds, and seasonings. Cook for 2-4 minutes, then remove and drain.

3. In a large bowl add chopped vegetables, pasta, beans, corn, ranch dressing, and zesty Italian dressing. Mix well and enjoy!

Rainbow Garden Salad

INGREDIENTS

1 Bag of Romaine Lettuce

1Lb Cherry Tomatoes

2 Cucumbers

1 Red Onion

1 Green Bell Pepper

1 Red Bell Pepper

1 Orange Bell Pepper

1 Yellow Bell Pepper

1 Tsp Salt

1 Tsp Black Pepper

Salad Dressing of Choice

DIRECTIONS

1. Cut up all the vegetables, add salt, and pepper, and mix in a large bowl. Add salad dressing of choice.

Enjoy!

Sweet Macaroni Tuna Salad

INGREDIENTS

1 Box Elbow Macaroni

4 Cans of Tuna Fish

3 Boiled Eggs

1 Stick of Celery (Diced)

1 Onion (Diced)

1 Green Bell Pepper (Diced)

4 Tbs Relish

½ Tbs Dijon Mustard

4 Tbs Mayonnaise

½ Tsp Ranch Dressing

1 Tbs Seasoning Salt

1 Tbs Black Pepper

1 Tbs Onion Powder

½ Tsp Paprika

1 Tbs Sugar

1 Tbs Salt

DIRECTIONS

1. In a medium pot add water and salt, then bring to a boil. Add macaroni and cook for 7-8 minutes. Remove from heat and strain under cold water. Then set aside.

2. In a large bowl add tuna, diced boiled eggs, relish, mustard, mayonnaise, ranch dressing, seasoning salt, black pepper, onion powder, paprika, sugar, onion, celery, bell pepper, and pasta. Mix well and place in refrigerator for half an hour to chill. Then serve and enjoy!

Sweet & Tasty Hawaiian Tuna Macaroni Salad

INGREDIENTS

1 Box Macaroni

4 Cans of Tuna Fish

½ Red Onion (Diced)

1 Carrot (Shredded)

½ Red Bell Pepper (Diced)

½ Orange Bell Pepper (Diced)

½ Yellow Bell Pepper (Diced)

½ Cucumber (Diced)

½ Celery Stick (Diced)

1 Tsp Seasoning Salt

1 Tsp Black Pepper

1 Tbs Sugar

1 Tbs Relish

2 Tbs Mayonnaise

1 Bottle of Minato's Hawaii Dressing

DIRECTIONS

1. In a medium pot add water and salt, then bring to a boil. Add macaroni and cook for 7-8 minutes. Remove from heat and strain under cold water. Then set aside.

2. In a large bowl add pasta, tuna, seasonings, relish, vegetables, mayonnaise, and Hawaii dressing. Mix well and refrigerate for half an hour.

Serve and enjoy!

Sweet And Spicy Seafood Macaroni Salad

INGREDIENTS

4 Cans Lump Crab Meat

2 Packs of Imitation Crab Meat

½Lb Scallops

2lbs Medium Peeled Shrimp

1 Box Macaroni Pasta

1 Tbs Salt

½ Cup Olive Oil

1 Tsp Red Pepper Seeds

1 Tbs Seasoning Salt

1 Tbs Black Pepper

1 Tsp Paprika

1 Tsp Old Bay Season

2 Tbs Sugar

1 Tsp Celery Seeds

2 Carrots (Shredded)

1 Stick Celery (Diced)

1 Red Onion (Diced)

1 Tsp Ranch Dressing

1 Cup Mayonnaise

1 Tbs Spicy Mustard

DIRECTIONS

1. In a medium pot add water and salt, then bring to a boil. Add macaroni and cook for 7-8 minutes. Remove from heat and strain under cold water. Then set aside.

2. In a medium frying pan add oil and heat on medium heat. Cook shrimp for 3-4 minutes then remove and set aside. In the same frying pan add scallops and sprinkle black pepper over scallops. Cook for 2-3 minutes on both sides then remove and set aside. Lastly, mix seasoning salt to lump crab meat, add to the frying pan, and cook for 15-20 minutes. Remove and set aside.

3. In a large bowl add imitation crab meat and break it into small pieces. In the same bowl add pasta, seasonings, vegetables, mayonnaise, mustard, shrimp, scallops, lump crab meat, and ranch dressing. Mix well, cover, and refrigerate for half an hour.

Serve and enjoy!

Macaroni Shrimp Salad

INGREDIENTS

2Lb Extra Large Peeled Shrimp

4 Cups Macaroni

2 Tbs Relish

1 Tbs Yellow Mustard

1 Tbs Seasoning Salt

1 Tbs Black Pepper

1 Tbs Garlic Powder

1 Tbs Onion Powder

1 Tsp Paprika

1 Tbs Sugar

1 Tbs Old Bay Seasoning

1 Cup Mayonnaise

3 Boiled Eggs (Diced)

½ White Onion (Diced)

½ Green Bell Pepper (Diced)

½ Stick Butter

DIRECTIONS

1. In a medium pot add water and salt, then bring to a boil. Add macaroni and cook for 7-8 minutes. Remove from heat and strain under cold water. Then set aside.

2. In a medium frying pan add butter and heat on medium heat. Season shrimp with old bay and cook for 3-4 minutes. Remove and set aside.

3. In a large bowl add pasta, seasonings, vegetables, boiled eggs, mayonnaise, mustard, relish, and shrimp. Mix well, cover, and refrigerate for half an hour.

Serve and enjoy!

Vegetarian Salad

INGREDIENTS

1 Cucumber

½ Lb Cherry Tomatoes

1 Can Corn

1 Can Black Beans

1 Can Red Kidney Beans

1 Can Chickpeas

1 Green Bell Pepper (Diced)

1 Yellow Bell Pepper (Diced)

1 Red Bell Pepper (Diced)

1 Orange Bell Pepper (Diced)

½ Red Onion (Diced)

1 Tsp Seasoning Salt

1 Tsp Black Pepper

½ Cup Zesty Italian Dressing

½ Tbs Mayonnaise

DIRECTIONS

1. Cut each tomato in half and add to a large bowl. Peel and cut up cucumbers, then add cucumbers and diced vegetables to the same bowl. Add dressing and mayonnaise and mix well. Set it aside.

2. In a medium pot add corn, black beans, kidney beans, chickpeas, black pepper, and seasoning salt. Cook for 6 minutes then remove and drain. Set it aside.

3. Add corn, beans, and chickpeas to vegetables. Mix well, cover, and refrigerate for half an hour.

Serve and enjoy!

Spicy Bean Salad

INGREDIENTS

2 Heads Romaine Lettuce (Chopped)

½ Head Radicchio (Chopped)

½ White Onion (Diced)

½ Red Onion (Diced)

1 Celery Stalk (Chopped)

½Lb Cherry Tomatoes (Halves)

½ Cup Buttered Flavored Hot Peppers

1 Cup Sun Dried Tomatoes (Chopped)

1 Can Black Beans

½ Cup Cubed Provolone Cheese

1 Tsp Salt

1 Tsp Black Pepper

Dressing:

½ Cup Extra Virgin Olive Oil

½ Cup Red Wine Vinegar

1 Tsp Honey

1 Tsp Minced Garlic

1 Tsp Dried Oregano

1 Tbs Black Pepper

1 Tsp Salt

DIRECTIONS

1. In a small pot add beans, salt, and pepper, and cook for 3-5 minutes. Remove, drain, and set aside.

2. In a small bowl add all dressing ingredients and mix well. Set it aside.

3. In a medium bowl add vegetables, cheese, hot peppers, beans, and dressing. Mix well and serve.

Enjoy!

Vegan Protein Salad

INGREDIENTS

1 Cup Broccoli (Chopped)

1 Cucumber (Diced)

1 Cup Romaine Lettuce

½ Cup Avocado (Diced)

½ Cup Zucchini (Diced)

½ Cup Organic Seasoned Croutons

½ Can Chickpeas

½ Cup Vegan Ranch Dressing

DIRECTIONS

1. In a small pot cook chickpeas for 3-4 minutes. Remove from heat and drain.

2. Mix all ingredients well.

Serve and enjoy!

Vegetarian Cucumber & Tomato Salad

INGREDIENTS

3 Lg Tomatoes (Chopped)

3 Cucumbers (Chopped)

½ Tbs Fresh Parsley

½ Cup Feta Cheese

2 Tbs Minced Garlic

2 Tbs Olive Oil

1 Tsp Salt

1 Tsp Black Pepper

Salad Dressing of Your Choice

DIRECTIONS

1. In a large bowl mix all ingredients together.

    Serve and enjoy!

BONUS RECIPES

Rich Girl Sausage Hoagie

INGREDIENTS

½ Onion (Chopped)

½ Green Bell Pepper (Chopped)

1 Tomato (Sliced)

3 Cups Romaine Lettuce (Shredded)

1 Fresh Roll

1 Tsp Cajun Seasoning

½ Cup Mayonnaise

1 Tsp Olive Oil

1 pack of Beef Kielbasa Sausage

DIRECTIONS

1. In a frying pan add oil and heat. Cut sausage in half and add to the frying pan. Cook for 7-9 minutes on both sides. Remove and set aside.

2. Add onions and peppers to the same frying pan. Cook for 2-3 minutes then remove and set aside in a small bowl. Split the roll and add to the frying pan. Let brown for 2-3 minutes, then remove.

3. In another small bowl add mayonnaise and cajun seasoning and mix well. Then spread the mixture onto the roll and add sausage, onions, peppers, lettuce, and tomato.

Happy Cooking!

Turkey Spaghetti With Red Sauce

INGREDIENTS

1 Box Spaghetti
1Lb Fresh Ground Turkey
1 White Onion (Diced)
½ Red Bell Pepper (Diced)
½ Green Bell Pepper (Diced)
½ Orange Bell Pepper (Diced)
1 Fresh Garlic (Crushed)
1 Tsp Hot pepper Flakes
½ Cup Fresh Parsley
1 Tbs Basil
½ Tsp Italian Seasoning
1 Tsp Salt
½ Tsp Pepper
1 Tbs Sugar
1 Tbs Garlic Powder
½ Cup Olive Oil
4 Cups Water
Sauce:
1 Cup Water
1 Tbs Worcestershire Sauce
15oz Tomato Sauce
1 Can Diced Tomato
1 Can Tomato Paste
1 Tbs Sugar
1 Tsp Salt
1 Tsp Black Pepper

DIRECTIONS

1. In a large skillet add oil and heat.

2. In a medium bowl add ground turkey, all peppers, onions, garlic, pepper flakes, ½ Tsp salt, and the remainder of the seasonings. Mix well then add to skillet. Cook for 14-15 minutes.

3. In a large pot add tomato sauce, diced tomato, tomato paste, worcestershire sauce, sugar, water, salt, and black pepper. Mix well and cook for 5-6 minutes. Remove from heat and set aside.

4. In a medium pot add water and salt, then bring to a boil. Add pasta and cook for 7-8 minutes. Remove from heat and strain under cold water. Then set aside.

5. In the large pot with sauce, add pasta and ground turkey mix. Mix and heat for 30 minutes.

Serve and enjoy!

Rich Flavor Cheeseburger

INGREDIENTS

½ Lb Ground Beef

1 Tsp Salt

1 Tsp Black Pepper

1 Tsp Old Bay

1 Tsp Lemon Pepper

2 Tbs Avocado Oil

1 Onion (Chopped)

3 Slices American Cheese

2 Round Rolls

½ Head Lettuce (Shredded)

½ Tomato (Sliced)

½ Tsp Russian Dressing

DIRECTIONS

1. In a medium bowl add ground beef, salt, old bay, and lemon pepper. Mix well and set aside.

2. In a medium frying pan add oil and heat. Add onions and black pepper and cook for 2-3 minutes. Remove and set aside.
   Add ground beef to the same frying pan and cook for 15-16 minutes. Drain as much excess oil off as you can and set aside.

3. Open rolls and add dressing, ground beef, onions, cheese, lettuce, and tomatoes.

Serve and enjoy!

Tasty Italian Cheeseburger

INGREDIENTS

1Lb Italian Ground Sausage

½ Cup Onion (Diced)

1 Egg

3 Red Roasted Bell Peppers (Diced)

1 Orange Roasted Bell Pepper (Diced)

½ Tbs Basil

½ Tbs Seasoning salt

½ Tbs Black Pepper

½ Tsp Garlic Powder

½ Tsp Onion Powder

½ Cup Avocado Oil

4 Hawaiian Sweet Rolls

4 Slices American Cheese

½ Cup Romaine Lettuce (Shredded)

½ Tomato (Sliced)

3 Tbs Mayonnaise

DIRECTIONS

1. In a medium bowl add ground beef, egg, onion, and seasonings. Mix well and set aside.

2. In a medium frying pan add oil and heat. Add bell pepper and cook for 2-3 minutes. Remove and set aside.

3. Create four patties with the ground beef mixture then add the patties to the same frying pan. Cook for 6-8 minutes on both sides. Then add cheese to the top of the patties while in the frying pan. Allow cheese to melt then remove and set aside.

4. Open each roll and add mayonnaise, cheeseburger, lettuce, bell peppers, and tomatoes.

Serve and enjoy!

Lemon Pepper Bbq Baby Back Ribs

INGREDIENTS

½Lb Pork Baby Back Ribs

1 Bottle Honey BBQ Sauce

2 Tbs Lemon Pepper

1 Tbs Garlic Powder

1 Tbs Onion powder

1 Tbs Smoked Paprika

1 Tbs Black Pepper

1 Tbs Brown Sugar

1 Tbs Basil

1 Tbs Italian Seasoning

½ Cup Olive Oil

Non-Stick Cooking Spray

DIRECTIONS

1. Preheat oven to 360 degrees. Cover a large baking pan with aluminum foil and spray it down with non-stick cooking spray. Set it aside.

2. In a medium bowl add all seasoning and oil. Mix well and rub down ribs front and back.
   Place ribs on the baking pan and cover with foil. Place ribs in the oven for one hour. Then turn the ribs over and place them back in the oven uncovered for another half hour.
   Add BBQ sauce to ribs and allow it to cook for another 20 minutes. Remove and set aside to cool. Then serve and enjoy.

Banging Lemon Pepper Pork Chops

INGREDIENTS

6 Pork Chop

1 Tbs Lemon Pepper

1 Tbs Garlic Powder

1 Tbs Onion Powder

1 Tbs Paprika

1 Tbs Basil

1 ½ Cup Olive Oil

1 Tbs Black Pepper

1 Tbs Parsley

½ Tsp Lemon Zest

Non-Stick Cooking Spray

DIRECTIONS

1. Preheat oven to 360 degrees. Cover a medium baking pan with aluminum foil and spray it down with non-stick cooking spray. Set it aside.

2. In a large bowl add oil, lemon zest, and all seasonings. Mix well and rub down pork chops front and back.
Place pork chops on the baking pan and cook for one hour uncovered. Then remove and allow to cool.

Serve and enjoy!

www.ingramcontent.com/pod-product-compliance
Lightning Source LLC
Chambersburg PA
CBHW041117120626
46547CB00019B/2749